Utah

BY ANN HEINRICHS

Content Adviser: Bonnie Rogers, Curator of Education, Utah State Historical Society, Salt Lake City, Utah

Reading Adviser: Dr. Linda D. Labbo, Department of Reading Education, College of Education, The University of Georgia

COMPASS POINT BOOKS ◈ MINNEAPOLIS, MINNESOTA

Compass Point Books
3109 West 50th Street, #115
Minneapolis, MN 55410

Visit Compass Point Books on the Internet at *www.compasspointbooks.com*
or e-mail your request to *custserv@compasspointbooks.com*

On the cover: Delicate Arch, Arches National Park near Moab

Photographs ©: Buddy Mays/Travel Stock Photography, cover, 1, 7; Digital Vision, 3, 36, 42; Unicorn
Stock Photos/Frank & Seth Hilberg, 5; Unicorn Stock Photos/Ron Holt, 6; Unicorn Stock Photos/Robert
Baum, 8; Steve Mulligan Photography, 10, 29; Unicorn Stock Photos/Robert E. Barber, 11; Unicorn Stock
Photos/Mark E. Gibson, 12; Richard Hamilton Smith, 13; Hulton/Archive by Getty Images, 14, 16 (top),
19, 46; North Wind Picture Archives, 15; Stock Montage, 16 (bottom), 17, 18, 41; Corbis/Scott T. Smith,
20; Photo Network/Grace Davies, 21; John Elk III, 23, 24, 35, 38, 43 (top); Corbis/AFP, 25; Jo Prater/
Visuals Unlimited, 26; Unicorn Stock Photos/H. H. Thomas, 27; Larry Ditto/KAC Productions, 28;
Bachmann/The Image Finders, 30, 48 (top); Tom & Therisa Stack/Tom Stack & Associates, 31, 47; Getty
Images/Brian Bahr, 33; Tom Walker/Visuals Unlimited, 34; Mark E. Gibson/The Image Finders, 39, 45;
David Falconer, 40; Robesus, Inc., 43 (state flag); One Mile Up, Inc., 43 (state seal); James P. Rowan, 44
(top); Inga Spence/Visuals Unlimited, 44 (middle); PhotoDisc, 44 (bottom)

Editors: E. Russell Primm, Emily J. Dolbear, and Patricia Stockland
Photo Researcher: Marcie C. Spence
Photo Selector: Linda S. Koutris
Designer: The Design Lab
Cartographer: XNR Productions, Inc.

Library of Congress Cataloging-in-Publication Data
Heinrichs, Ann.
  Utah / by Ann Heinrichs.
      p. cm. — (This land is your land)
  Summary: Describes the geography, history, government, people, culture, and attractions of Utah.
Includes bibliographical references (p.) and index.
  ISBN 0-7565-0344-2 (hardcover : alk. paper)
  1. Utah—Juvenile literature. [1. Utah.] I. Title.
  F826.3 .H45 2004
  979.2—dc21   2002151670

Table of Contents

NOTE: In this book, words that are defined in the glossary are in **bold** the first time they appear in the text.

Welcome to Utah!

Brigham Young led a religious group of settlers westward in 1847. They were Mormons—members of the Church of Jesus Christ of Latter-day Saints. Life had been hard for them in eastern states. Many Mormons were treated badly and even killed. They hoped to find a place to live in peace.

At last they reached the Salt Lake Valley in present-day Utah. Brigham Young, sick with fever, looked out across the valley. "This is the right place," he declared. "Drive on!"

The Mormons worked hard to build communities in Utah. They developed farming, ranching, and iron and coal mining **industries.** Brigham Young preached against gold, silver, and copper mining. Today, Utah produces goods ranging from computers to space equipment. Ranches are still thriving, and minerals continue to be valuable state resources.

Many visitors enjoy Utah for its natural wonders. They love its sweeping deserts and snowcapped mountain peaks.

Amazing rock formations tower high above the landscape. Their red, pink, and purple colors glisten in the sun. Now come explore this land of wonders called Utah.

▲ **East of Moab, rock formations tower over a ranch along the Colorado River.**

Mountains, Deserts, and Canyons

Utah is located in the western United States. It's shaped like a box with a notch cut out of the northeast corner. All of Utah's borders are perfectly straight lines. Idaho and Wyoming lie to the north. Nevada is to the west, and Colorado is to the east. South of Utah is Arizona.

▲ **Colorful sandstone formations rise throughout the Colorado Plateau.**

▲ **Flaming Gorge Reservoir on the Green River**

Southern and eastern Utah are part of the Colorado **Plateau.** Colorful cliffs, arches, and other rock formations rise throughout this region. Wind and water formed them over millions of years. Rivers have carved canyons through the rock. Much of this area is preserved as national parks and monuments.

The Green River courses through eastern Utah. One of its canyons, Flaming Gorge, reaches into Wyoming. In southern Utah, the Green River flows into the Colorado River. A dam

The Wasatch Mountains are located in northeastern Utah.

on the Colorado forms huge Lake Powell in Glen Canyon. This lake crosses the border into Arizona.

Northeastern Utah is in the Rocky Mountain region. Its major mountain ranges are the Wasatch and Uinta Mountains. The base of the Wasatch Mountains is called the Wasatch Front, or the Salt Lake Valley. This has always been Utah's most heavily settled area. Streams running down from the mountains made it a fertile farming region. Today, a large cluster of cities stretches along the Wasatch Front. The biggest is Salt Lake City, which is also the state capital.

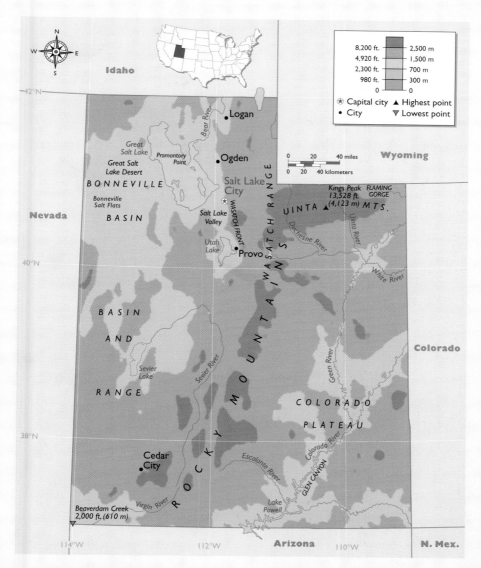

Idaho

Nevada

40°N

38°N

Logan

Great Salt Lake
Great Salt Lake Desert
BONNEVILLE
Bonneville Salt Flats
BASIN

Promontory Point

Ogden

Salt Lake City

Salt Lake Valley

WASATCH FRONT

Utah Lake

Provo

BASIN

AND

Sevier Lake

RANGE

Sevier River

Cedar City

Beaverdam Creek 2,000 ft. (610 m)

Virgin River

Escalante River

Lake Powell

GLEN CANYON

Colorado River

COLORADO PLATEAU

WASATCH RANGE

UINTA

Kings Peak 13,528 ft. (4,123 m)

FLAMING GORGE

MTS.

Duchesne River

Uinta River

White River

Green River

ROCKY MOUNTAINS

Wyoming

Colorado

N. Mex.

Arizona

114°W   112°W   110°W

42°N

Bear River

8,200 ft.	2,500 m
4,920 ft.	1,500 m
2,300 ft.	700 m
980 ft.	300 m
0	0

⊛ Capital city   ▲ Highest point
• City   ▽ Lowest point

0   20   40 miles
0   20   40 kilometers

N
W   E
S

▲ **A topographic map of Utah**

The Basin and Range region covers western Utah. It's a region of dry, flat lowlands. Small mountains rise here and there. Northwestern Utah is often called the Bonneville Basin.

▲ **The Bonneville Salt Flats in Tooele County are part of the Great Salt Lake Desert.**

It's named for Lake Bonneville, an ancient freshwater lake that once covered this area. As the lake slowly dried up, minerals and salts were left behind.

Today, Utah's Great Salt Lake is what's left of Lake Bonneville. Its waters are saltier than any ocean in the world. South and west of the lake is the Great Salt Lake Desert. Part of this desert is called the Bonneville Salt Flats. This broad stretch of gleaming white land has a rock-hard surface.

Elk, moose, and pronghorn antelopes roam freely across Utah. The mule deer is

▲ **Mountain goats live on Utah's rocky hillsides.**

the most common large animal in the state. The mountain forests shelter foxes, bobcats, coyotes, raccoons, rabbits, weasels, and many other types of animals. Mountain sheep and mountain goats scamper across the rocky hillsides. Prairie dogs and porcupines are found in Utah, too. Snakes, horned lizards, and tortoises live in the desert regions. Gila monsters, which are lizards with a poisonous bite, live in this part of the southwest.

The California gull, the state bird, nests on islands in the Great Salt Lake. Gulls saved settlers' crops in 1848. They ate

▲ **A ski resort in Alta**

the Rocky Mountain crickets that swarmed into the area. The honeybee is the state insect. For Mormons, honeybees are a symbol of hard work.

Utah is one of America's driest states. Little rain falls in the deserts and lowlands. Heavy summer rainstorms sometimes strike quickly in the south and east. Water gushes through the canyons, causing floods and **landslides.** The high mountains and plateaus get the most snow. In winter, Utah's mountains are popular spots for skiing and other winter sports.

A Trip Through Time

People have lived in present-day Utah since 11,000 B.C., about 13,000 years ago. The first residents of Utah were the Paleo-Indians. Later, the Archaic **Culture** joined the Paleo-Indians. These people were nomadic, moving from place to place in order to hunt and gather food. Around the year A.D. 400, the ancient Pueblo and Fremont Cultures grew in northern and eastern Utah. Like the earliest Utahns, they hunted and gathered, but they were not nomadic. They built homes and grew their own food.

At about the same time, the ancient Pueblo people moved into southeastern Utah. They built houses in the sides of cliffs and valleys. These houses were like apartment buildings for many families.

▲ The ancient Pueblo people lived in cliff dwellings.

▲ Members of the Shoshone tribe dressed in the same clothes as the Mormons who lived in Salt Lake City in 1872.

The ancient Pueblo people raised corn, beans, and squash. They wove baskets and made pottery and clay figures.

Later, many Native American groups moved in. These groups were united by different versions of the Shoshone language. The four main Native American groups were the Ute, the Southern Paiute, the Goshute, and the Northern Shoshone. The Ute people lived in central and eastern Utah. The state is named after these people. There were different groups of Ute peoples. Utes in the east hunted buffalo across the plains. Others used **irrigation** to grow corn and pumpkins.

White settlers later called the Utes of southwestern Utah the Southern Paiute. The Southern Paiute were peaceful people who hunted, farmed, and gathered plants. The Goshute lived in the western deserts and collected seeds, grasses, roots, and insects to eat. They also hunted deer and rabbits. The Northern Shoshone hunted and gathered food on the northeastern plateaus. During the early 1700s, another group of Native Americans called the Navajo began to move into Utah from the south. They settled in the southeastern part of the state. The Navajo often came in conflict with the Ute people.

Spanish explorers from Mexico traveled through Utah in 1776. However, they made no settlements there. British and American trappers and fur traders entered Utah during the 1820s and 1830s. They made several trails through the Wasatch Mountains and drew maps of the area. A trapper named Jim Bridger passed through Utah in 1824. He was probably the first white person to see the Great Salt Lake.

▲ Trapper Jim Bridger traveled through Utah in 1824.

▲ Morman leader
Brigham Young

▲ Some Mormon pioneers
made the journey to Utah in
covered wagons.

Utah's first permanent white settlers were Mormons seeking religious freedom. Mormon leader Brigham Young led settlers into the Great Salt Lake region in 1847. They called their new land *Deseret,* a word from the Book of Mormon meaning "honeybee." Using irrigation, the new settlers were able to farm in the desert. They set up busy communities throughout the region.

Thousands of newcomers arrived along a route called the Mormon Trail. Some came in covered wagons. Others traveled on foot with carts they pulled or pushed by hand. Utah passed from Mexico to the United States

▲ Riders for the Pony Express delivered mail between Missouri and California.

in 1848, and Utah Territory was created in 1850. The new territory's governor was Brigham Young.

The Pony Express began service in Utah in April 1860. Expert riders who worked for this speedy mail service galloped between Missouri and California delivering mail.

In 1861, a **telegraph** line was completed in Salt Lake City. It was the country's first **transcontinental** telegraph. Thanks to this invention, people could send messages more quickly between the Atlantic and Pacific coasts than if they used mail. As a result, the Pony Express went out of business.

▲ Crowds gathered in 1869 to witness the meeting of the Union Pacific and Central Pacific Railroads in Promontory.

The first transcontinental railroad line was also completed in Utah. In 1869, eastern and western sections of the railroad met in Promontory.

The U.S. government was slow to grant statehood to Utah. Many government leaders disapproved of Mormon beliefs and customs. Some Mormons practiced polygamy, which is the custom of having more than one wife. Beginning in 1862, Congress passed several laws against polygamy. During the 1880s, hundreds of Utah's Mormons were jailed for breaking these laws. Then Utah drew up a constitution, or set of basic laws, that outlawed polygamy. In 1896, Utah finally joined the Union as the forty-fifth state.

During the early 1900s, Utah's industries grew. New irrigation systems opened more land to farming, and railroads connected Utah with other parts of the country. Mining became a big industry, too. Mines took metals such as silver, gold, coal, lead, copper, and iron from the ground. Many smelters opened. Their blazing furnaces separated the metal from other minerals. At one point, the American Smelt-

▲ A copper mine in Bingham Canyon in 1942

ing and Mining Company's smelter in Murray produced more metals than any other smelter in the world.

The Great Depression of the 1930s was hard on Utahns. More than one out of three workers in the state lost their jobs. Utah's industries recovered during World War II (1939–1945). Farms, factories, and mines produced much-needed supplies

▲ **Recycled scrap metal is used to manufacture steel at this mill in Plymouth.**

for the war effort. Hill Air Force Base became an important supply center for the United States armed forces.

After World War II, the U.S. government began building missiles in Utah. Government industries, farming, and copper mining are still important to the state. Busy factories also make computers and office machines. Tourism is one of the biggest industries in Utah. The ski slopes of Utah's mountains, as well as the scenic beauty of its many national and state parks, draw many visitors. Utahns struggle to keep a balance between industry and **conservation.** They hope to preserve Utah's natural beauty for years to come.

Government by the People

In 1983, fifth-graders in Salt Lake County were studying how their state government works. They were also learning about honeybees. The students knew that the honeybee was an important symbol for Utah. They also knew that Utah had no official state insect at that time.

The students wrote to the state lawmaker for their region. They explained why the honeybee would be the perfect state insect for Utah. The lawmaker was impressed and introduced a bill, or suggested law, to all the other lawmakers. The bill would make the honeybee Utah's state insect. The lawmakers agreed with the fifth-graders and voted yes! This is a great example of government in action. Utah's state government works just like the U.S. government. The governing power is split into three branches—legislative, executive, and judicial.

▲ The honeybee is Utah's state insect.

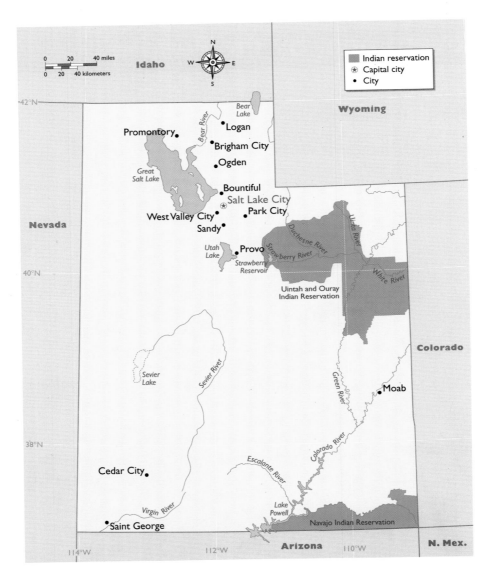

Idaho

Wyoming

Nevada

Colorado

Arizona

N. Mex.

Indian reservation
⊛ Capital city
• City

42°N
40°N
38°N
114°W
112°W
110°W

Bear Lake
Bear River
Promontory
Logan
Brigham City
Ogden
Great Salt Lake
Bountiful
Salt Lake City
West Valley City
Sandy
Park City
Utah Lake
Provo
Strawberry River
Strawberry Reservoir
Duchesne River
Uinta River
White River
Uintah and Ouray Indian Reservation

Sevier Lake
Sevier River
Green River

Moab

Cedar City

Escalante River
Colorado River
Lake Powell
Virgin River
Saint George
Navajo Indian Reservation

▲ **A geopolitical map of Utah**

The legislative branch makes state laws. Voters elect their politicians to serve in the state legislature. It has two houses, or sections—the twenty-nine-member senate and the seventy-five-member house of representatives.

The job of the executive branch is to see that laws are obeyed. Utah's governor heads the executive branch. The state's voters elect their governor to a four-year term. They also elect several other executive officers, including the lieutenant governor and the attorney general. No executive officer may serve more than twelve years in a row.

Judges and their courts make up the judicial branch. The judges study the law and decide if someone has broken it. Utah has different types of courts. The highest court is

▲ **The state capitol in Salt Lake City**

the state supreme court. Its five justices, or judges, serve ten-year terms. The governor appoints each new supreme court judge. After that, voters decide whether a judge should serve another term.

Utah is divided into twenty-nine counties. Voters in each county elect a county commission or county council. They also elect county officers such as the sheriff.

Within each county are cities and towns. A town is a community with fewer than 800 people. Many cities and towns choose a mayor or manager and a city council. Some cities elect commissioners. In certain towns, voters elect a town council.

What do nurses, computer programmers, and restaurant cooks have in common? They are all service workers. They sell something very valuable—their special skills. Service industries are Utah's biggest business. Service workers may have jobs in hospitals, banks, or government offices. Others might work in repair shops, ski resorts, or neighborhood stores.

▲ With the help of her bomb-sniffing dog, a police officer checks luggage at the airport in Salt Lake City. Police officers are service workers.

▲ Workers at this Utah well pump valuable oil from the ground.

Utah's leading factory goods are related to transportation. That includes transportation in space! Factories near Salt Lake City and Brigham City manufacture parts for spacecraft. Computers and other electronics are also important products. Other factories make food products, metal goods, chemicals, and machines.

Copper was once Utah's leading mineral. Today, Utah produces more copper than any state besides Arizona. However, petroleum (oil) is now Utah's most valuable mining product. Coal, natural gas, silver, and gold are some of the state's other minerals.

The Great Salt Lake is rich in magnesium and several types of salts. Table salt does not come from the Great Salt Lake because it would not be pure enough to put on your food. However, there are many other kinds of salts. For example, Utah's potassium salts are made into fertilizer. The salt that is put on icy roads in the winter often comes from the Great Salt Lake.

How do people get the salts from the Great Salt Lake? They use solar energy, or "sun power." First, they collect lake

▲ A salt mine near the Great Salt Lake

▲ Cows graze in a pasture in Zion National Park in Springdale.

water in huge, shallow ponds. As the sun shines on the ponds, the water evaporates, or changes from liquid to vapor. With the water gone, the salts are left behind.

Most of Utah's farmland is used for grazing beef and dairy cattle. Beef cattle and milk are the state's top farm products. Utah farmers also raise turkeys, chickens and eggs, hogs, and sheep.

Utah's major crops are hay, wheat, barley, potatoes, onions, and corn. Important fruits are apples, peaches, pears, apricots, and cherries. Among all the states, Utah ranks third in its production of apricots and fifth in its production of tart cherries.

Vast regions of Utah have almost no residents. Most people settled in the Salt Lake Valley. About three out of five Utahns live in the area stretching from Provo to Ogden. Salt Lake City, the state capital, is Utah's largest city. Next in size are West Valley City, Provo, and Sandy. In population, Utah ranks thirty-fourth among all the states. More than 2 million people lived there in 2000.

Almost nine out of ten Utahns have European **ancestors.** Most came from England and Scandinavia. Others arrived from Germany, Ireland, Greece, Italy, and other countries. **Hispanics,** Asians, Native Americans, Polynesians, and African-Americans live in Utah, too.

▲ **Provo is Utah's third-largest city.**

The Navajo, Ute, Goshute, Southern Paiute, and Shoshone are Utah's five existing Native American groups. Many live on the state's Indian **reservations.** The Uintah and Ouray Reservation covers a huge area in eastern Utah. The Navajo Reservation in the southeast spills over into other states.

Salt Lake City is the world headquarters for the Mormon church. Today, about seven out of ten Utahns are Mormons. Joseph Smith of New York founded the religion in 1830. According to Smith, an angel named Moroni revealed God's teachings to him. Smith wrote down these teachings in the Book of Mormon.

▲ **Children play on the Navajo reservation in Monument Valley.**

Mormon beliefs and customs shape much of Utah's culture. Mormon values include a close-knit family life, hard work, and clean living. Hundreds of Mormon churches, called ward houses, have been constructed throughout Utah.

▲ **The Mormon temple in Temple Square in Salt Lake City**

Many large cities have tabernacles and temples. There are ten tabernacles and temples in Utah. Salt Lake City's Mormon Tabernacle Choir is world famous.

Education is important to Utahns. Utah is one of the highest-ranking states in high school graduates and college students. Utahns also rank high in literacy—the ability to read and write. Utah's first university, the University of Deseret, was established in 1850. It was later renamed the University of Utah. Brigham Young University (BYU) in Provo was founded by Brigham Young in 1875.

Pioneer Day in Utah is July 24. Mormon pioneers first arrived on that day in 1847. Today, Utahns celebrate the event all over the state. The biggest festival is Salt Lake City's Days of '47. Its parade is one of the biggest in the country. The town of Bountiful holds Handcart Days. It honors the thousands of Mormons who traveled to Utah with handcarts.

Have you ever heard of the Golden Spike? It was a big, golden nail that was hammered in to complete the transcontinental railroad in 1869 at Promontory. Every May, Utahns reenact this event at Promontory Summit.

Utah's Native Americans hold powwows and tribal gatherings around the state. They celebrate their culture with traditional music and dance.

Movie star Robert Redford founded the Sundance Institute in Park City. It helps filmmakers learn and practice their art. Thousands of movie fans attend the Sundance Film Festival every January.

Sports fans around the world had their eyes on Utah in 2002. That's when Salt Lake City hosted the Winter

▲ Skiers from Germany, Norway, and France celebrate during the 2002 Winter Olympic Games in Salt Lake City.

Olympic Games. Even without the Olympics, Utah has an exciting sports life. The Utah Jazz is the men's basketball team. Fans know they can usually count on the Jazz to reach the National Basketball Association (NBA) playoffs. Utah is also home to the Salt Lake City Stingers, a minor league baseball team, and the Utah Grizzlies, a minor league hockey team.

Where would you find hoodoos and fins? You'll see hundreds of them in Bryce Canyon National Park. They are some of the park's fantastic rock formations. Wind and water shaped them over millions of years. Some hoodoos look like tall, ghostly figures. Paiute Indians called them Legend People.

Another strange Utah landform is the Waterpocket Fold. It's a giant wrinkle in Earth's crust. Capitol Reef National Park

▲ **Rock formations at Bryce Canyon National Park**

▲ **Waterpocket Fold in Capitol Reef National Park is a giant wrinkle in Earth's crust.**

preserves the fold's colorful cliffs and canyons. Massive stone arches stand in Arches and Zion National Parks.

Several ancient Native American cliff dwellings survive in southern and eastern Utah. Hovenweep National Monument is on the Navajo Reservation. Pueblo people built its stone towers and houses hundreds of years ago.

How long is your shadow late in the day? To see a *really* long shadow, visit Monument Valley in southeastern Utah. A rock formation there called the Totem Pole has a shadow that is 35 miles (56 kilometers) long at sundown! Other awesome formations in the valley are named Mittens, Three Sisters, and Ear of the Wind.

▲ **The sandstone formations of Monument Valley in southeastern Utah**

Can you float in a swimming pool? In the Great Salt Lake, you'll float without even trying. The lake contains much more salt than the ocean. The salt makes the water dense, or heavy. You float because your body is less dense than the water.

Do you like to watch race cars? Then head out to the Bonneville Salt Flats. They're west of the Great Salt Lake. High-speed cars are tested there to see how fast they can go.

Salt Lake City, Utah's capital, is full of historic sites. Many important buildings stand around Temple Square. One is the magnificent Mormon Temple. Only Mormons may enter this house of worship. Another is the dome-shaped Mormon

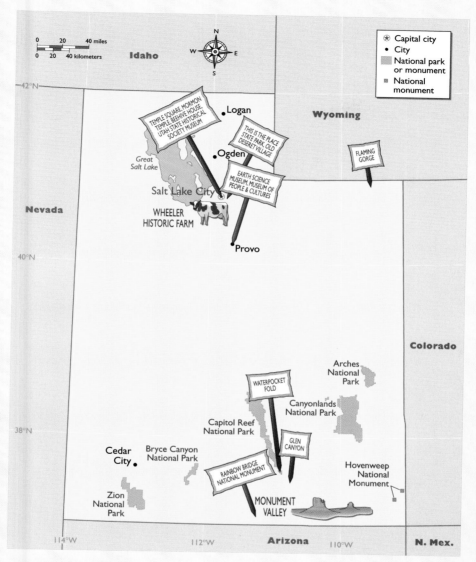

Scale:
0 20 40 miles
0 20 40 kilometers

N W E S (compass)

Idaho

Wyoming

42°N

Logan

TEMPLE SQUARE MORMON TEMPLE, BEEHIVE HOUSE, UTAH STATE HISTORICAL SOCIETY MUSEUM

THIS IS THE PLACE STATE PARK, OLD DESERET VILLAGE

FLAMING GORGE

Great Salt Lake

Ogden

EARTH SCIENCE MUSEUM, MUSEUM OF PEOPLE & CULTURES

Nevada

Salt Lake City

WHEELER HISTORIC FARM

40°N

Provo

Colorado

Arches National Park

WATERPOCKET FOLD

Canyonlands National Park

Capitol Reef National Park

38°N

GLEN CANYON

Cedar City

Bryce Canyon National Park

Hovenweep National Monument

RAINBOW BRIDGE NATIONAL MONUMENT

Zion National Park

MONUMENT VALLEY

114°W

112°W

Arizona 110°W

N. Mex.

▲ **Places to visit in Utah**

Tabernacle, with its massive pipe organ. Nearby is the Beehive House. This mansion was Brigham Young's home. The copper-domed state capitol displays historical exhibits. The Utah State

Historical Society Museum also has exhibits on Utah's pre-history, explorers, mountain men, early settlements, mining and railroad industries, and inventions such as the television and artificial heart.

Plum Alley was once the center of Salt Lake City's Chinese community. Chinese immigrants came to Utah to work on the railroads and stayed to labor in the mines during the 1800s. The Salt Lake City and County Building is decorated with carvings of Native American chiefs, Spanish

▲ **The Beehive House in Salt Lake City**

explorers, and Mormon pioneers—all important figures in Utah's history.

▲ Visitors explore an early pioneer settlement at the Pioneer State Park.

This Is the Place State Park is a special location to many Utahns. According to legend, Brigham Young arrived here in 1847. He looked out from this point and declared, "This is the place"—the spot where his followers could finally settle. The park's Old Deseret Village has both historically preserved and re-created buildings to show what life was like during Utah's early days. At Wheeler Historic Farm, you can take a tractor-drawn wagon ride and visit with the animals.

How would you like to see a 150-million-year-old dinosaur egg? Better yet, how would you like to see what's inside it? Just visit the Earth Science Museum at BYU in Provo. There you'll see a computer scan of the big egg. It shows the baby dinosaur that was developing inside. The museum also has complete dinosaur skeletons. The Utah Museum of Natural

▲ A bicyclist enjoys a trip through one of Utah's scenic recreation areas.

History is another fun place to view dinosaur exhibits. BYU also operates the Museum of Peoples and Cultures. It features the history and culture of people around the world.

Dams created two of Utah's best recreation areas—Flaming Gorge and Glen Canyon. These are good spots for boating, fishing, water skiing, and swimming. Maybe you'd rather hike the rugged trails. Along the way, you'll see amazing views of brilliant red cliffs and canyons. You may even catch a glimpse of herds of antelope along the shores. In some places, ancient ruins remind you that people lived there long ago. In other spots, you get the feeling that no one has ever been there before. Either way, you'll agree that Utah is a great place to explore!

Important Dates

1776   Fathers Francisco Atanasio Dominguez and Silvestre Velez de Escalante explore Utah.

1824– 1825   Trapper Jim Bridger reaches the Great Salt Lake.

1847   Brigham Young brings Mormon pioneers to Utah.

1848   Utah passes from Mexico to the United States.

1849   Mormons establish the State of Deseret.

1850   Utah Territory is established.

1861   The transcontinental telegraph is connected in Salt Lake City.

1867   The Mormon Tabernacle opens in Salt Lake City.

1869   The transcontinental railroad is completed at Promontory.

1870   *Salt Lake Tribune* newspaper is established.

1890   Mormon leaders advise members not to practice polygamy.

1896   Utah becomes the forty-fifth U.S. state on January 4.

1913   The Strawberry River Reservoir is completed.

1913   Zion National Park is established.

1952   Uranium is discovered near Moab.

1950s   Utah becomes a center for making missiles.

1964   Flaming Gorge Dam on the Green River and Glen Canyon Dam in Arizona open.

1985   U.S. senator Jake Garn of Utah is the first public official to travel in space.

1999   A tornado causes serious damage in downtown Salt Lake City.

2002   Salt Lake City hosts the Winter Olympic Games.

Glossary

ancestors—a person's grandparents, great-grandparents, and so on

conservation—protecting the land, water, air, and wildlife

culture—a group of people who share beliefs, customs, and way of life

Hispanics—people of Mexican, South American, and other Spanish-speaking cultures

industries—businesses or trades

irrigation—a way of bringing water to fields through canals or ditches

landslides—the washing away of hillsides caused by heavy rains

plateau—high, flat lands

reservations—large areas of land set aside for Native Americans

telegraph—a system for sending messages using a code of electrical signals that are sent over a wire

transcontinental—stretching across an entire continent

Did You Know?

★ Rainbow Bridge is the world's largest bridge of natural rock. It stands 290 feet (88 meters) high and measures 275 feet (84 m) across.

★ Utah has five national parks—Arches, Bryce Canyon, Canyonlands, Capitol Reef, and Zion.

★ The U.S. government owns more than half of Utah's land. These federal lands include national parks, forests, and monuments.

★ The Great Salt Lake is the largest natural lake west of the Mississippi River.

★ More than thirty movies have been filmed in Utah's Monument Valley. Many are Westerns, such as *How the West Was Won, Once Upon a Time in the West,* and *She Wore a Yellow Ribbon.*

★ In 1970, Gary Gabelich set a land-speed record at the Bonneville Salt Flats. He drove his jet-powered car an average of more than 622 miles (1,001 kilometers) per hour.

State capital: Salt Lake City

State motto: Industry

State nickname: Beehive State

Statehood: January 4, 1896; forty-fifth state

Land area: 82,168 square miles (212,814 sq km); **rank:** twelfth

Highest point: Kings Peak, 13,528 feet (4,123 m)

Lowest point: Beaverdam Creek in Washington County, 2,000 feet (610 m) above sea level

Highest recorded temperature: 117°F (47°C) at Saint George on July 5, 1985

Lowest recorded temperature: –69°F (–56°C) at Peter's Sink on February 1, 1985

Average January temperature: 25°F (–4°C)

Average July temperature: 73°F (23°C)

Population in 2000: 2,233,169; **rank:** thirty-fourth

Largest cities in 2000: Salt Lake City (181,743), West Valley City (108,896), Provo (105,166), Sandy (88,418)

Factory products: Transportation equipment, electronics, food products

Farm products: Beef cattle, milk

Mining products: Petroleum, copper, coal, natural gas

State flag: Utah's state flag shows a shield within a gold band upon a field of blue. In the center of the shield is a beehive, the state emblem. It represents hard work and industry. On each side of the beehive are sego lilies, the state flower and a symbol of peace. Above the hive is the state motto, "Industry." Beneath it is the word *Utah*. Below the shield is the date 1847, the year the Mormons arrived in Utah. Above the shield is an American eagle with arrows in its claws. That stands for protection in peace and war. American flags curve from the eagle's wings to the bottom. They stand for Utah's support for America. At the bottom is the date 1896, the year of Utah's statehood.

State seal: The state seal has the same design and symbols as the state flag. Around the border are the words "The Great Seal of the State of Utah" and the date 1896.

State abbreviations: Utah or Ut. (traditional); UT (postal)

State Symbols

State bird: California gull

State flower: Sego lily

State tree: Blue spruce

State animal: Rocky Mountain elk

State fruit: Cherry

State vegetable: Spanish sweet onion

State historic vegetable: Sugar beet

State fish: Bonneville cutthroat trout

State insect: Honeybee

State mineral: Copper

State rock: Coal

State gem: Topaz

State grass: Indian rice grass

State fossil: Allosaurus

State emblem: Beehive

State star: Dubhe

State folk dance: Square dance

State cooking pot: Dutch oven

Making Tart Cherry Pie

Tart cherries are Utah's delicious state fruit.

Makes eight to ten servings.

INGREDIENTS:

1 1/2 cups sugar

4 tablespoons quick tapioca

3 cans tart cherries (14 1/2-ounce cans)

2 ready-made pie crusts, unbaked

2 tablespoons margarine, cut into pieces

DIRECTIONS:

Make sure an adult helps you with the hot oven and the cutting. Preheat the oven to 400°F. Mix sugar and tapioca in a large mixing bowl. Drain cherries, add, and stir. Line a deep pie plate with one pie crust. Spread the mixture in it. Place pieces of margarine on top. Place the other pie crust on top. Trim to fit, and mash the edges together with a fork. Cut cherry outlines on the top, cutting all the way through the crust. Place the pie on a baking sheet. Bake 45 to 50 minutes, or until crust is golden brown. Cool on a wire rack. For an extra treat, serve with ice cream on top.

State Song

"Utah . . . This is the Place"

Words by Sam Francis and Gary Francis; music by Gary Francis

Utah! People working together
Utah! What a great place to be.
Blessed from Heaven above.
It's the land that we love.
This is the place!
Utah! With its mountains and valleys.
Utah! With its canyons and streams.
You can go anywhere.
But there's none that compare.
This is the place!

It was Brigham Young who led the pioneers
   across the plains.
They suffered with the trials they had
   to face.
With faith they kept on going till they
   reached the Great Salt Lake
Here they heard the words..."THIS IS
   THE PLACE!"

Utah! With its focus on family,
Utah! Helps each child to succeed.
People care how they live.
Each has so much to give.
This is the place!

Utah! Getting bigger and better.
Utah! Always leading the way.
New technology's here...
Growing faster each year.
This is the place!

There is beauty in the snow-capped
   mountains, in the lakes and streams.
There are valleys filled with farms and
   orchards too.
The spirit of its people shows in everything
   they do.
Utah is the place where dreams come true.

Utah! With its pioneer spirit.
Utah! What a great legacy!
Blessed from Heaven above.
It's the land that we love.
This is the place!

Utah! Utah! Utah!
THIS IS THE PLACE!

Roseanne Barr (1952–) is a comedian and actress. She starred in her own television show, *Roseanne.* Barr was born in Salt Lake City.

Wilford Brimley (1934–) is an actor. Some of his movies include *The China Syndrome* (1979), *The Natural* (1984), and *The Firm* (1993). He was born in Salt Lake City.

Butch Cassidy (1866–1908?) was an outlaw who robbed banks and trains. He was born Robert LeRoy Parker in Beaver.

Philo T. Farnsworth (1906–1971) invented the television and the electronic microscope. Farnsworth was born near Beaver.

Edwin Jacob ("Jake") Garn (1932–) served as a U.S. senator from Utah from 1975 to 1993. In 1985, he became the first politician in space when he flew aboard the space shuttle *Discovery.* Garn was born in Richfield.

Karl Malone (1963–) is a star player for the Utah Jazz basketball team. He is nicknamed "the Mailman" because he can deliver winning plays. Malone was born in Louisiana.

J. Willard Marriott (1900–1985) founded the Marriott chain of restaurants and hotels. He was born at Marriott Settlement near Ogden.

Peter Skene Ogden (1794–1854) was a fur trapper and trader. He explored the Salt Lake area. The river and city of Ogden were named after him. Ogden was born in Quebec, Canada.

Donny Osmond (1957–) and **Marie Osmond** (1959–) are a brother and sister who act, sing, and dance. They hosted television's *The Donny and Marie Show.* The Osmonds were born in Ogden.

Ivy Baker Priest (1905–1975) was the U.S. treasurer from 1953 to 1961. Priest was born in Kimberly.

Wallace Stegner (1909–1993) was an author who taught at the University of Utah. His book *The Gathering of Zion* (1964) describes the journey along the Mormon Trail. Stegner was born in Iowa.

James Woods (1947–) is an actor and a movie producer. Woods was born in Vermal.

Brigham Young (1801–1877) was president of the Church of Jesus Christ of Latter-day Saints (Mormon Church). He brought Mormon settlers to Utah and founded Salt Lake City. Young (pictured above left) was born in Vermont.

Loretta Young (1913–2000) was an actress who appeared in almost 100 movies. She also hosted television's *Loretta Young Show.* Young was born in Salt Lake City.

Want to Know More?

At the Library

Joseph, Paul. *Utah*. Edina, Minn.: Abdo & Daughters, 1998.

Lassieur, Allison. *The Utes*. Mankato, Minn.: Bridgestone Books, 2002.

McCormick, Nancy, and John McCormick. *Discovering Utah*. Salt Lake City, Utah: Peregrine Smith Books, 1986.

Neri, P. J. *Utah*. Danbury, Conn.: Children's Press, 2002.

Rambeck, Richard. *Utah Jazz*. Mankato, Minn.: Creative Education, 1998.

Sirvaitis, Karen. *Utah*. Minneapolis: Lerner, 1991.

Thompson, Kathleen. *Utah*. Austin, Tex.: Raintree/Steck-Vaughn, 1996.

On the Web

Welcome to Utah!
http://www.utah.gov
To visit the state web site and learn about Utah's history, government, economy, and land

Utah Adventure Travel
http://www.utah.com
To find out about Utah's events, activities, and sights

Utah State Historical Society
http://history.utah.gov
To learn more about Utah's history

Through the Mail

Utah Travel Council
P. O. Box 147420
Salt Lake City, UT 84114
For information on travel and interesting sights in Utah

Utah Department of Community and Economic Development
324 South State Street, Suite 500
Salt Lake City, UT 84111
For information on Utah's economy

Utah State Historical Society
300 South Rio Grande
Salt Lake City, UT 84101
For information on Utah's history

On the Road

Utah State Capitol
300 North State Street
Salt Lake City, UT 84114
801/538-3000
To visit Utah's state capitol

Index

About the Author

Ann Heinrichs grew up in Fort Smith, Arkansas, and lives in Chicago. She is the author of more than one hundred books for children and young adults on Asian, African, and U.S. history and culture. Ann has also written numerous newspaper, magazine, and encyclopedia articles. She is an award-winning martial artist, specializing in t'ai chi empty-hand and sword forms.

Ann has traveled widely throughout the United States, Africa, Asia, and the Middle East. In exploring each state for this series, she rediscovered the people, history, and resources that make this a great land, as well as the concerns we share with people around the world.